The Star 3000

by James Clements
Illustrated by Emily Fox

OXFORD
UNIVERSITY PRESS

adult

All was <u>calm</u> and quiet in the house. Dad was out at the shops. Mum was relaxing on the sofa reading a book, and Joel was doing his homework. He was looking up facts about sharks for a project at school.

As usual, things didn't stay <u>calm</u> in the house for long.

It was very <u>calm</u> in the house; no one was being noisy or excitable. When are you most <u>calm</u>? When are you most excited?

child

Dad burst in to the room.

Look! Look in my bag!

3

adult

Dad pulled out a box and placed it on the table <u>beside</u> Joel.

"Ta-dah! It's called the Star 3000. You can ask it anything, and it finds the answer on the Internet. It's brilliant!" shouted Dad.

"Hmm, perhaps …" said Mum.

Can you point to the box <u>beside</u> Joel in the picture on this page? Are you sitting <u>beside</u> anyone at the moment?

child

You might need this.

No!

adult

"Are you sure you don't want to read the instructions?" said Joel. "You might miss something important."

"Don't worry," said Dad. He pushed the plug into the socket, and the Star 3000 came to life with a loud bleep. "Now, let's test it," said Dad, excitedly. "The Star can help you with your homework, Joel. Ask it for a fact about sharks!"

child

Star, tell me a shark <u>fact</u>!

Arctic sharks cut food with a sharp tooth.

Joel asks the Star 3000 for a <u>fact</u>. Can you explain what a <u>fact</u> is? You might say: *A <u>fact</u> is something that is …*

adult

"It works!" exclaimed Dad.

"Just one tooth?" said Joel. "Is that right? I thought sharks had lots of sharp teeth …"

"Of course it's right! The Star said so," cried Dad.

"Hmm, perhaps …" said Joel.

"It's brilliant! Ask the Star for another fact, Joel," shouted Dad, jumping up and down on the spot.

Perhaps means *possibly* or *maybe*. Do you think Joel is sure that the Star's facts are correct, or is he not completely sure?

child

Star, tell me a shark fact!

Sharks hunt chips.

Do *you* think the Star 3000 is telling Joel a correct fact this time? Do *you* think it is true?

adult

"That doesn't sound right at all!" said Joel. "There are no chips in the sea!"

"Are you sure the Star's facts are correct, Dad?" asked Mum.

"Yes!" exclaimed Dad. "The Star is brilliant!"

To exclaim means to say something loudly, in surprise or excitement. Can you exclaim 'Yes!' like Dad does on this page?

child

Star, tell me a shark fact!

Sharks can snarl and moo, too.

adult

"Sharks don't moo!" said Joel. "Are you sure that you set the Star up properly, Dad?"

"Hmm, let's give it another <u>chance</u>," said Dad.

Dad wants to give the Star 3000 another <u>chance</u>. Do you think it will give a real fact this time?

child

Star, tell me a shark fact!

You can look for sharks with fur at the farmyard.

13

adult

"These facts from the Star aren't right!" exclaimed Joel.

Mum looked across at Dad, raising one eyebrow.

"Hmm, perhaps …" said Dad.

Dad started to put the Star 3000 back into its box.

child

In the morning, Dad took the Star back to the shop.

Look at that!

Do you think that there is a chance that Dad will buy something else from the shop?

True or false?

Can you guess which shark facts below are true?

1) Sharks normally eat ...
   a) seashells
   b) other fish

2) Sharks have babies called ...
   a) pups
   b) kittens

3) Sharks have a good ...
   a) singing voice
   b) sense of smell

4) Some sharks have ...
   a) 15 rows of teeth
   b) 15 sleeps in a day

5) Sharks do not have ...
   a) bones
   b) fins

Answers: 1: b, 2: a, 3: b, 4: a, 5: a